C for Computer,
S for System

Are you too young to modern technologies and feeling like sometimes you can't even follow what is discussed on the internet? Or have you already seen some in school but are still feeling frustrated because there are still so many difficult languages you have never seen? In the modern digital era there are many new words and phrases popping up on a daily basis. These new language stuff tend to be flexible and way less formal. Still, they can become fairly easy to learn if there are straight forward explanations available to get you started. This is exactly what we have prepared for you here – plain-English introduction of the fundamental tech terms you need to know to survive the 21 century classroom.

This book focuses on computer systems related tech words and phrases.

Restrictions on Alteration

You may not modify the Book or create any derivative work of the Book or its accompanying documentation. Derivative works include but are not limited to translations.

Restrictions on Copying

You may not copy any part of the Book unless formal written authorization is obtained from us.

operating system

It is the most important program that runs on a computer. Every computer must have an operating system to run other programs. It performs all the basic tasks.

It is often being referred to as "OS".

All modern operating systems are multi-tasking and multi-user capable.

On a multi-user system, one user cannot interfere with another user's activities.

process

A process refers to a program being executed.

Each process has its own descriptive information structure known as process control block. This is something rather technical... .

root

If you are using Windows you do not need to know root.

In Unix and Linux, the root of the entire directory tree structure is called root.

root can also mean the mighty administrator of the system.

windows

The most popular operating system from Microsoft.

Most end user systems come equipped with Windows out of the box.

Windows has different versions. Windows 10 is for desktop. Windows Server is for server. And there are Windows versions for mobile devices.

unix, solaris and linux

Unix is an established operating system most commonly found on high end servers.

To run this system, special skills are required.

Solaris is a famous Unix implementation.

Linux is a Unix variant. It is quite common on middle end servers and workstations.

Many (but not all) Linux distributions are free of charge.

redhat and ubuntu

Redhat is a major enterprise grade Linux distribution.

It has different versions for desktop computers and servers. The focus, however, is always on enterprise grade servers.

ubuntu is another famous Linux distribution. It is for personal computers, while Ubuntu Touch is for tablets and smartphones.

nas and san

NAS network-attached storage is a server dedicated to file sharing and nothing else.

A SAN Storage Area Network is a high-speed network of shared storage devices which is available to all servers on the network.

nos

A NOS network operating system refers to a software based operating system that includes special functions for connecting computers and devices in a network.

it is primarily for supporting client computers. It provides printer sharing, file system and database sharing, application sharing, network management and security ...etc.

NOS runs mostly on server systems.

bootup

It refers to the process of loading an operating system on a computer as soon as the computer is turned on.

The boot process is required on all hardware devices that run an OS.

bug, patch and hotfix

A bug refers to a flaw in a program that can cause the computer to malfunction.

A patch refers to partial software program released by the software developer for fixing bugs.

A patch can fix one or more problems.

A hotfix is sort of a quick fix for targeting a specific problem in a software. It may or may not be distributed to the public.

driver and signed driver

A driver refers to the software program that controls your hardware or peripheral devices. Almost every hardware requires a driver in order to be usable by the operating system.

In Windows, a driver is called a device driver.

A signed driver refers to the software program that controls the hardware or peripheral devices. What makes it special is that it is associated with a digital certificate that can properly identify the publisher of the driver. This can ensure that you are not using something from some ill intended source.

client and server

To make things simple, just keep in mind an end user is always a client. A client always enjoys services provided by others.

A client can be a desktop computer, a notebook, a mobile phone or a pad device.

A server is a way more powerful and resourceful computer that is dedicated for providing services to you.

A regular user seldom needs to work directly on a server.

workstation and desktop

Powerful client computers equipped to do serial work such as drawing, animation, programming ... etc.

A desktop is a regular PC.

Generally, a workstation is more powerful than a desktop, even though in reality the gap is minimal.

Copyright 2020 **Tomorrowskills.com**.

peer and host

A peer is a member of a group of computers. These computers are of the same level - they can mutually support each others (that is what we call peer to peer).

By definition a peer can act as both a client and a server.

A host refers to a computer or any other device that can communicate with others on the network.

Technically, a client computer is a host. A server is also a host.

file system

It is a structure that keeps track of the way files are organized on the disk drive. You can think of it as a hierarchical collection of files and directories that make up an organized, structured set of stored information you can retrieve if needed or wanted.

disk drive

It allows you to store data on the computer system.

The basic physical construction of a hard disk drive consists of spinning disks with read/write heads that move over the disk surfaces to store and read data.

A system can have multiple drives.

sata

SATA Serial Advanced Technology Attachment is a standard hardware interface for connecting drives to the computer.

Most modern PCs use SATA hard drives. The good thing about SATA is that it uses very thin cables. The problem with thick cables is that they fill up the chassis and block air flow.

raid

RAID = redundant array of inexpensive drives.

A RAID configuration can provide additional protection against data loss by mirroring the data on multiple hard disks, thus protecting yourself from disk failure. The more disks a server has the better the redundancy.

ssd

Solid state drive. Solid state refers to electronic circuitry that built with semiconductors for serving as the primary storage medium instead of magnetic media.

It is very fast. It is also pretty small in physical size.

It is relatively more expensive though.

flash card

Flash memory media (such as CF card and SD card) uses a special type of solid state memory chip that requires no power to maintain its contents. Flash memory can be easily moved from digital cameras to notebook or desktop computers and can even be connected directly to photo printers or self-contained display units.

cdrw and dvdrw

A CD-ROM (compact disk read-only memory) is an optical read-only storage medium based on the original digital audio format first developed for audio CDs. Other formats such as CD-R, or CD recordable, and CD-RW, or CD rewritable, are basically the "writable" version of this form of storage medium.

processor, processor core and clock rate

AKA CPU, this central processing unit is the heart of a computer in which arithmetic and logical operations are performed and instructions are decoded and executed.

It controls and manages the entire operation of the computer.

You can think of a multicore processor as multiple processors being integrated into one single chip. In theory, more cores means more processing power.

Clock rate typically refers to the frequency at which the processor runs.

clock speed and ghz

Clock speed measures how fast a computer can complete basic computations and operations.

The processor speed in ghz indicates the speed at which a processor can complete a certain amount of cycles per second.

One gigahertz means one billion cycles completed per second. This is now the most popular processor speed measurement unit.

bios and cmos

BIOS stands for Basic Input/Output System, which is stored in ROM. BIOS is the first group of instructions that are available when the computer is turned on.

It is used by the startup routine to check out the system

CMOS = Complementary etal-oxide semiconductor. It is a read-only memory chip for storing data that is read by the BIOS so as to obtain information on hardware configuration.

intel, i3, i5, i7, i9 and amd

Intel is the dominant processor manufacturer.

Most server computers use Intel processors.

i3 has 2 physical cores and 2 virtual cores.

Since i5 there are minimum 4 physical cores.

i7 and i9 are real high end processors.

AMD is another processor manufacturer. Many gaming computers use AMD processors.

x86 and x64

Originally x86 refers to the instruction sets supported by the processor. Nowadays it usually refers to the Intel processor family.

x86 is 32 bit. X64 is 64 bit.

All modern operating systems can support 64 bit processors! They are faster and more scalable.

cooler and heatsink

A processor must have a heat sink and a cooling fan attached, otherwise it will get overheated. It is not uncommon to have thermal grease applied in between the processor and the heatsink to make heat dissipation more effective.

High end gaming computers often use water cooler for the best possible cooling effect.

turbo boost

It is a technology implemented by Intel only. It can be found in certain versions of their Core i5 and Core i7 processors. The feature enables an Intel based processor to run above its base operating frequency.

memory

AKA RAM, Random Access Memory is a required component - data is being processed while being stored temporarily in RAM. Upon completion of processing, data is moved from RAM to disk drive for long term storage.

In theory, more RAM means faster processing since it works faster than disk drive.

caching

It can speed up information exchange since an up-to-date copy of frequently used information is kept in the closest location. The memory area for caching is called a cache.

Modern processors have cache built-in for performance improvement.

system bus and pci-e

It refers to the communication system that allows data to flow between components inside a computer.

The higher the bus speed the better in general.

PCI-E is a BUS standard primarily for powerful graphic display card.

graphic card and gpu

A device which handles screen display. Lower end computers have graphic card integrated into the system's motherboard. Higher end cards are usually separated.

GPU = graphics processing unit. It is a specialized chip built into the graphic card for manipulating video memory and speeding up the building of images.

ATI and Nvidia are the most famous brands in graphic chipsets.

ATI is now part of AMD, a competitor to Intel.

lcd/led

Liquid crystal display LCD is a flat display panel. LED screen is LCD that makes use of a series of Light Emitting Diodes to backlight the panel. Simply put it is a more advanced display technology.

The traditional "monitor" is completely extinct.

dvi and hdmi

DVI shorts for Digital Visual Interface. It is a special video connector designed by the Digital Display Working Group for maximizing picture quality of digital projectors and LCD screens.

HDMI shorts for High-Definition Multimedia Interface. It is a digital interface that can be used with a HDTV to produce the best uncompressed digital picture possible. It sends audio and video signal in one cable, and is much faster than DVI.

refresh rate and resolution

The time it takes for a monitor's electron beam to draw the screen from top to bottom depends on how high the refresh rate is.

It usually ranges from 60 to 80 Mhz.

Resolution is the method of measurement for the detail level of images produced by a display panel. It is measured by a horizontal and vertical number of pixels.

kvm

A KVM switch is a special kind of hardware device that allows one to control multiple computers from a single set of keyboard, video display and mouse. This reduces the need for purchasing multiple input sets and displays.

nvidia, geforce, ati and radeon

Nvidia is a very famous brand of graphic chipsets. Most modern 3D games support its chipsets (known as GEFORCE).

ATI is another very famous brand of graphic chipsets. Most modern 3D games also support its chipsets (known as RADEON).

AMD acquired ATI in 2006. Ryzen is a new line of AMD processors with ATI Radeon graphics integrated.

chipset

It refers to a set of electronic components in an integrated circuit that work together to manage the data flow between the processor, the memory and the various components.

usb

USB = Universal Serial Bus. It allows many devices to be simultaneously connected to a single port.

You can also use USB hub to connect multiple USB devices to a single USB port.

controller

It refers to the hardware device that manages the flow of data between components. Disk controller controls disk drive. I/O controller controls input/output devices ...etc.

integrated peripherals

These are the functions integrated into the motherboard. Onboard controller, onboard sound, onboard video... etc.

In the past these functions are all separated. Nowadays the trend is to have everything built onboard.

motherboard and integrated circuit

It refers to the mainboard of the computer system. The processor and the RAM modules all sit on this board.

A motherboard is an example of integrated circuit board.

ddr and gb

Dynamic random-access memory. This usually refers to the memory modules of the computer. Video cards use DDR memory as well.

GB shorts for Gigabyte. This is the measurement unit for RAM and smaller storage.

For server system, 16GB RAM is minimum while 32GB is more common. For computer desktop, 4GB RAM is the absolute minimum standard nowadays.

tb

Terabytes. This is the measurement unit for modern storage. A 1TB drive seems to be the modern day minimum.

We do not yet have 1tb of RAM for desktop computers.

ports, parallel and com ports

In the context of computer hardware, ports can be used for connecting external devices directly to the computer. USB port is the most common today.

In the context of computer hardware, parallel port is mostly for printer. It is quite legacy.

Com port is mostly for mouse and modem. It is quite legacy.

power supply

The basic function of a power supply is to convert the type of electrical power available at the wall socket to the type that computer circuitry can use. The power supply in a conventional desktop system is designed to convert either 115 volt or 230 volt AC power into 12 volt DC power.

modem, printer and network printing

Modem can be internal or external. You use it to make slow internet connection or to send fax. It is quite legacy.

You use a printer to produce hard copies out of your computer files. The major types of printers include laser printer, inkjet printer, dot matrix printer and thermal printer.

Network printing means the printer is not directly attached to the computer. Printing is done through network connection.

inkjet, laser and postscript

Inkjets use liquid ink-filled cartridges.

Laser printer are toner based. There is a photosensitive drum serves as the core of the electro-photographic process.

Postscript is a page description language in the electronic and desktop publishing areas.

scanner, ppi and dpi

A scanner is a computer device that can read printed text graphics and translate the information into a form the computer can read and store.

Scanner works by digitizing an image.

Scanner resolution is measured in pixels per inch ppi. It describes the resolution in the unit of pixels.

Dots per inch is a measure of spatial printing / video dot density in the number of individual dots that can be placed within the span of a linear inch. This value often indirectly correlates with image resolution.

flatbed and handheld scanners

A flatbed scanner is composed of a glass pane, under which there is a bright light which illuminates the pane, and a moving optical array in scanning.

A handheld scanner is a manual device that is dragged across the surface of the image to be scanned.

ocr

To edit text scanned by the scanner, you need to use an optical character recognition OCR system to translate the image into text characters that can be read by your word processors. The scan resolution determines the file size and quality.

log in, log on and sign in

It means the "sign in" action. Normally you must have registered an account first in order to sign into a computer system, unless the system is completely unprotected.

login

It may refer to the credentials you use to sign in, particularly your login name. In most cases the login is your account name.

It may also indicate the sign in action. It is quite common for computer systems to display a login button for you to click and proceed to logging in.

account

Most networked computer systems require that you first register an account in order to log in and use the services provided. Account registration involves asking you to fill in a bunch of information and specify an account name for yourself. This may be done manually by the administrator or via other means.

log off, logout and sign out

They mean the same thing. You usually do this when you are about to stop using the computer.

See this example: I logged off so that John could use the computer.

Sometimes a user can be logged off by an administrator for security purpose.

lockout

This usually means "account lockout". That is, you are being logged off (which may be against your will) by someone who has administrative power over your account.

Copyright 2020 **Tomorrowskills.com**.

console

This term can refer to a network capable gaming device (a game console) or simply a combination of input and output methods (console input via keyboard and output via monitor). A router can have a console connection (they call it terminal emulation).

Sometimes a terminal may be referred to as a console.

ios and MacOS

When written as iOS, it refers to the mobile operating system created and developed by Apple Inc. exclusively for its own hardware products.

When written as IOS, it may refer to the operating system created and developed by Cisco Inc. exclusively for its own router hardware products.

MacOS is not the same as ios. MacOS runs on Mac based desktop computers.

.NET

It is a framework for software development framework. Microsoft offers this framework as a controlled programming environment where software can be developed. It is Microsoft proprietary. Some software require this framework in order to run. You can download it for free from Microsoft anyway.

cable and cabling

Technically this word can mean many things. In the context of internet connection, cable connection is one type of high speed access, typically provided by the local cable TV provider.

Sometimes people use this word to describe computer that does not connect through wireless means.

Sometimes the term "cabling" refers to the transmission media of the network. Sometimes it refers to the act of setting up cable connections for a network.

vm

VM shorts for virtual machine.

It is an emulation of a computer system. Technically it is a computer file (aka an image) that works like an actual physical computer. It is easier to install and maintain and is more cost efficient than running multiple separate physical computers.

A physical computer can run multiple VMs simultaneously.

Modern servers are always based on VMs.

END OF BOOK

*Please email your questions and comments
to admin@Tomorrowskills.com.*

www.ingramcontent.com/pod-product-compliance
Lightning Source LLC
LaVergne TN
LVHW052313060326
832902LV00021B/3865